VIVIWAVA

Tales from the Islands

JORDAN DEAN

Text copyright © Jordan Dean

Illustrations copyright © Tamara Jenkinson

First Edition: June, 2018

The moral right of the author has been asserted.

Published by JDT Publications
Port Moresby, NCD, Papua New Guinea
Email: jdtpublications@gmail.com

National Library of Papua New Guinea
Cataloguing-in-Publication entry:

Dean, Jordan. 1984 — .
    Viviwava: Tales from the Islands.

ISBN-13: 978-9980-901-70-5

    1. Tales, Papua New Guinea. 1. Short Stories (English).
PNG/398.209541/D42 – dc22

Printed in USA by CreateSpace Independent Publishing.

The stories in this anthology were retold by my uncles;
Saul Tony, John Paul, Frank Paul and aunty Margret Saul
This book is dedicated to you.

In loving memory of my late grandfather Tony Bokialei.
May our stories live on.

Many thanks to;
Chips Mackellar and Ed Brumby for the editorial support
Tamara Jenkinson for the beautiful illustrations.

Special thanks to;
Dr. Trish Nicholson for the superb Foreword
Maleta Tokwakasi for the lovely cover photograph.

CONTENTS

Jordan Dean

FOREWORD

I feel honoured to be writing a few words to herald this gem of Papua New Guinea's rich storytelling culture. Though the stories evoke the islands of Milne Bay, where they have been passed down for generations, their importance is far wider. Folk tales inspire, instruct, and entertain, but there is more to them than this.

Like all folk tales, the myths, legends and fables in Viviwava contain layers of meaning, their wisdom released through many retellings. People grow with their stories, as stories grow with their people. It is through stories that we understand ourselves and the world around us, near and far.

We should all listen to stories from everywhere. But the tales of our own people, our own culture, are seeds of our identity, they nourish our soul.

If we do not know our own stories, we lose who we are and cannot connect with others. That is the special significance of this beautiful anthology as a shining example to us all to preserve and share our stories with others.

Dr. Trish Nicholson
Social Anthropologist and Author.
A Biography of Story, A Brief History of Humanity
Inside the Crocodile: the Papua New Guinea Journals

PREFACE

Viviwava in my native Miapuna language means tales, legends, fables or myths. For many years, the sharing of stories, mythology, fables and legends has helped to create and maintain our unique cultures.

Our stories explained our beliefs about the world, taught moral principles or were simply told for the sake of entertainment.

The stories in this anthology originate from the D'Entrecasteaux Islands of Milne Bay Province in Papua New Guinea. For years, the stories have been passed down through generations by word of mouth. Our oral tradition of storytelling has always been an important way to preserve our culture and heritage.

It is important for our children to have some kind of connection to their place of origin; be it by birth or family heritage.

I hope readers will find this anthology enjoyable and perhaps challenging.

Jordan Dean
June, 2018

GABUBU – LEGEND OF THE WHITE DOVE

Winner of the Heritage Writing – Crocodile Literature Prize, 2017

Long, long ago, on Fergusson Island, there once lived a white dove named Gabubu. His younger brother was a parrot named Gewala. The two brothers would go out every night, prowling for young ladies together. As usual, Gewala was sent to wake the ladies up.

Gabubu was a very handsome white dove. All the young ladies loved Gabubu and rejected the other birds. That made the other birds jealous.

One day, Gabubu and Gewala were sitting by the shore. The cool sea breeze made Gabubu fall asleep. The other birds flew in and quickly tied up Gabubu's wings and loaded him in a canoe.

"If you tell anyone, we will kill you," the other birds threatened Gewala.

Gewala watched helplessly as the other birds pushed the canoe out to sea and it drifted away. He mourned for his elder brother. "My brother, Gabubu. My brother, Gabubu. May the stars protect you and may the winds take you to an island and wash you ashore there."

His mother heard Gewala's cry from the garden. She flew out to sea and landed on the outrigger of the drifting canoe. Upon seeing Gabubu's wings tied up, she wept. "I warned you not to look for ladies. Now, the other birds became jealous and did this to you. I am too old and cannot remove the ropes they tied you with. But, I will never leave you, my son."

They continued drifting for a month without food and water. His mother got so weak and died at sea. Finally, the canoe drifted upon a deserted shore somewhere in Wedau.

A young lady saw the drifting canoe and swam out to it. Gabubu told her to collect all the feathers of his mother and put them in a coconut basket. She then cut the rope and released Gabubu.

The young lady took care of Gabubu until he regained his health. They got married and had a son.

His wife would spend every day working in the garden. Gabubu stayed at home with his son. He did nothing except sharpen wooden combs.

That made his wife angry and she yelled at him, "You lazy man! All you do is make combs as if those combs will give you food to eat. I should have left you to die with your mother."

Gabubu was upset with her words. He collected his mother's feathers and put them on his body. He flew up to a coconut tree frond to try his wings. Satisfied that he could fly, he hid the feathers.

The next day, Gabubu put on his mother's feathers and flew up to the coconut tree. When his wife returned from the garden, she found her son crying on the ground.

"Where is your father?" she asked her son, who kept crying and pointing up to the coconut tree.

She looked up and saw Gabubu sitting high up on the coconut tree's frond.

"Please don't leave me and your son here. Please come back, my husband," she cried to Gabubu.

"My son will replace me. Take care of him. When he grows up, he will make your garden, climb your coconut tree, catch your tuna and build your house. As for me, I shall return to my home," Gabubu said.

Gabubu flew to Girumea Point and stood on a coconut tree. He looked back at his wife and son for the last time.

"Goodbye," Gabubu said.

He waved at them and flew over the sea to his home, Fergusson Island.

And that's the reason why you'll find small white doves around the Wedau and Rabaraba area and big white doves on Fergusson Island.

Jordan Dean

MWATA'YALA – LEGEND OF THE LAKE PEOPLE

Finalist of the Heritage Writing – Crocodile Literature Prize, 2017

Once upon a time, two boys and a small girl lived beside a lake. A monster snake called Mwata'yala lived in the lake. Mwata'yala had eaten their parents and everyone in the village.

One day, the two boys went out fishing, leaving the small girl all by herself. The small girl climbed a frangipani to thread her necklace. While she was threading, she cried:

"My big brothers, you went out fishing and left me alone. Now Mwata'yala is coming to swallow me."

On hearing the small girl's cry, the monster snake replied:

"Ah, I am not here to swallow you. I came to see your tattoo and I will return."

She continued threading and cried again:

"My big brothers, you went out fishing and left me alone. Now Mwata'yala is coming to swallow me."

Again, the snake replied:

"Ah, I am not here to swallow you. I came to see your tattoo and I will return."

But the monster snake had lied. He slithered up the tree and swallowed the small girl.

Upon returning, her two brothers realised that Mwata'yala had taken their small sister. Furious, they planned to kill the monster snake.

"Spear the neck and the tail, but not the stomach," the eldest brother said.

The younger brother had a two-pronged spear. When they found the monster snake, the younger brother speared it in both eyes and it died.

They cut open the monster snake's stomach and released their small sister. They were happy to find her still alive. They embraced each other and cried.

And, from the small girl, the next generation of the lake people were born.

Jordan Dean

TONIMAGU

Published in the Crocodile Literature Prize Anthology, 2017

Once upon a time, there lived a small boy named Tonimagu, which means 'my hand'. His parents had died many years ago and his uncle had adopted him. They lived near the coast.

His uncle was a great fisherman. Every day, his uncle would go out fishing. When he returned, his aunty would cook the fish with garden food. His aunty would give the cooked food to her children to eat while Tonimagu was given only scraps and uncooked food to eat.

When Tonimagu tasted the uncooked food, he would go to the back of the hut and pour it out. Though hungry, he was punished by being made to work all day.

At night, when his uncle ate his dinner, Tonimagu would gape hungrily. His aunty would scold him saying, "Oh, you just finished eating your food and now you're watching your uncle eat. Go to sleep, Tonimagu."

Tonimagu would shed tears and go to sleep hungry. His life was miserable and he missed his parents so much. He wished his parents were still alive so he wouldn't be mistreated.

This went on and on until one day when his uncle returned from a fishing trip and dinner was cooked. As usual, Tonimagu was fed the uncooked food while his aunty and her children ate the cooked food. After dinner, his uncle smoked the leftover fish to preserve them.

As soon as everyone was fast asleep, Tonimagu crawled quietly to the fire place. Just as he reached out to grab a smoked fish, his uncle woke up. He pulled out his bush knife and cut Tonimagu's hand, thinking it was a dog attempting to steal the fish.

Tonimagu held his hand in pain, and blocked the bleeding with a piece of cloth. That night, he cried himself to sleep.

Early the next day, when the roosters were crowing, Tonimagu left the hut and followed the river upstream. At around midday, he sat on a flat rock to rest. He removed the cloth that covered the cut on his hand. He shook his hand and his blood splattered onto the nearby bushes. All sorts of food crops grew magically. On the flat rock, where he sat and where some of his blood had dripped, there grew a huge, giant taro.

Tonimagu continued further upstream until the sun was about to set. He looked around and fell in love with the place. He decided to settle there.

He removed the cloth again, shook his hand and again his blood splattered to the nearby bushes. Again, all sorts of food grew. Bananas, taro, yam, tapioca, sugar cane, pineapples, pumpkin, melons and all kinds of food grew magically.

For several weeks, his uncle searched for Tonimagu but couldn't find him. After some time, his uncle went out fishing and saw white smoke rising up from deep within the jungle. Seeing the smoke, his heart was troubled.

"That must be Tonimagu making fire in the jungle," his uncle muttered.

After fishing, his uncle paddled home slowly, still thinking about Tonimagu. He smoked the fish over the fire and went to sleep.

Early the next day, he put the fish in a coconut woven basket and set off in the direction of the smoke. He followed the river upstream until he reached the flat rock where Tonimagu had rested. He saw the giant taro and other food crops growing. He ate some ripe bananas before continuing upstream.

After some time he arrived at the place where Tonimagu lived. When he looked around, he couldn't believe his eyes. There were bananas, taro, yams, sweet potatoes, tapioca and all sorts of food growing everywhere.

Tonimagu was working in his garden. His uncle took a red berry from a nearby tree and threw it at Tonimagu.

Tonimagu jumped when the berry hit him. "Ah, which stupid bird dropped this berry on me?"

Tonimagu looked around but couldn't see anyone. He continued working on his garden. His uncle threw another berry.

"You silly birds! Why are you throwing these red berries at me?" Tonimagu shouted.

After the third berry hit him, Tonimagu studied the fruit carefully. "This looks like my uncle's finger prints," Tonimagu thought and looked around again.

His uncle came out of the bushes. Both of them hugged and cried for a long time. His uncle asked him why he ran away to live deep in the jungle. Tonimagu told him about how his aunty mistreated him, feeding him bones and uncooked food.

"You'll find the uncooked food at the back of the hut," he said to his uncle.

They had a delicious meal and went to sleep. The next day, Tonimagu harvested yams, taro and bananas and other food for his uncle to take back with him.

When his uncle arrived at his hut, he scolded his wife for mistreating Tonimagu.

"Every time I go out fishing, you feed my nephew with uncooked food. You made him upset and now he lives deep in the jungle."

After some time, there was a great famine on the island. Tonimagu's uncle went out fishing and smoked the fish. After loading the fish in coconut baskets, his uncle summoned his wife and their children and they all visited Tonimagu.

The children were so excited. They rushed for the ripe bananas, pineapples and melons. His uncle and aunty harvested yam, taro and banana from Tonimagu's garden. The next day, with all their coconut baskets filled with food, they returned to the coast.

When the food ran out, they decided to pay a visit to Tonimagu again. But when they tried to go upstream, a very steep mountain blocked their way. They cried and begged Tonimagu to remove the steep mountain. But Tonimagu paid no attention to their cries.

And so, they became hungrier and hungrier with every passing day until they all died.

KULELE AND THE MAGIC FLUTE

Long, long ago, on Goodenough Island, there lived a young man called Kulele. Kulele had sores all over his body. He lived in a small bush hut on a hill with his old mother. On a nearby island called Fergusson lived a very rich king. He had three beautiful daughters. The youngest was the loveliest and fairest. She had silky black hair and the most gracious heart. Her name was Lolee.

Kulele played his magical flute every night when the moon shone brightly. The coconut palm trees swayed, the seagulls danced and the ocean moaned to the melodies of his magical flute. The three princesses listened to the sweet melodies and yearned to marry the mysterious man playing the flute.

One day, the eldest princess asked her father.

"Father, I wish to travel to Goodenough Island to find the mysterious man who plays the flute."

"Very well, my eldest daughter. Take the sailing canoe with my best sailors," the king said.

The eldest daughter set sail for Goodenough Island. When she arrived at the shore, a horrible smell greeted her. The place stank like a dead corpse. She immediately ordered the sailors to return to the palace on Fergusson Island.

Upon seeing her elder sister return without success, the second born princess also asked her father.

"Father, I wish to travel to Goodenough Island to find the mysterious man who plays the flute."

"Very well, my second daughter. Take the sailing canoe with my best sailors," the king said.

The second born princess set sail for Goodenough Island. When she arrived at the shore, a horrible smell greeted her. Just as her elder sister had said, the place stank like a dead corpse. She too ordered the sailors to return to the palace on Fergusson Island.

Upon seeing her second sister also return without success, Princess Lolee, the youngest daughter asked her father. "Father, I wish to travel to Goodenough to find the mysterious man who plays the flute."

"Very well, my youngest daughter. Take the sailing canoe with my best sailors," the king said.

Princess Lolee set sail for Goodenough Island.

When she arrived at the shore, the same horrible smell greeted her. Unlike her elder sisters, she ignored the smell and climbed the hill and arrived at the little bush hut.

Kulele's mother greeted her. "Beautiful lady, what brings you here?"

"I came in search of the man who plays beautiful melodies every night. I wish to marry him," Princess Lolee said.

"Oh young lady, his name is Kulele and he's my son. However, he has sores all over his body that smell. You will not like him when you see him," Kulele's mother said.

"I don't care how stinky his sores are, I shall marry him," Princess Lolee insisted.

"Very well young lady. He is in the hut."

Princess Lolee met Kulele and fell in love with him. She nursed his sores and bathed him. She gave him new clothes to wear.

They then sailed back to Fergusson Island to meet the king. But when Princess Lolee asked for her father's blessings to marry Kulele, the king disowned her.

"Get this horrible smelling man out of my sight!" the king ordered.

Her elder sisters mocked her too. Embarrassed and humiliated, Princess Lolee and Kulele left the palace. They sheltered at a pigsty with the pigs.

Some months passed and the king decided to host a *singsing* and feast. The *singsing* would go on for a week. Word was sent far and wide for all the young men to attend in their best traditional costumes. The king intended to choose three of the best dancers to marry his three daughters. Princess Lolee told Kulele about the *singsing* and feast.

"You should attend the *singsing*. I'll just stay here with the pigs," Kulele said.

"No! I'll stay here with you," Princess Lolee said.

"I'll be fine. Please go and enjoy yourself," Kulele insisted.

On the day of the *singsing*, hundreds of pigs were killed and giant taro, bananas and yams were harvested from the gardens for the feast. Young men came from far and wide in their traditional costumes.

A conch shell was blown to herald the start of the *singsing*. The young men beat their *kundu* drums and danced back and forth. A young man appeared and asked Princess Lolee to dance with him.

He looked like a prince with an elegant headdress that had Bird of Paradise feathers. He was the most handsome man she had ever seen. Princess Lolee accepted and they danced together all night. Before dawn, the young man disappeared. Princess Lolee looked among the crowd but couldn't find him.

The sun rose and the dancers stopped to rest. Princess Lolee returned to the pig sty.

Kulele was up early. He had prepared breakfast and seemed to be in a happy mood.

"How was your night? Did any handsome man ask you for a dance?" Kulele asked.

"Oh, it was great. There was one man I danced with but I don't know his name," Princess Lolee said, feeling guilty.

"He must be very handsome. Too bad, I have sores all over my body and can't go to the *singsing* with you," Kulele said and smiled.

Princess Lolee felt that something was not right.

Why wasn't her husband jealous of her dancing with another man? And why did this mysterious handsome man disappear before dawn?

The *singsing* continued the next night. The same handsome man asked Princess Lolee to dance again. She danced with him. But her mind was troubled.

At around midnight, she quietly escaped from the *singsing* area and hurried back to the pig sty. Kulele was nowhere to be seen. She checked their room and found Kulele's skin with sores lying on the floor. Princess Lolee was filled with anger and threw the skin into the fire.

At dawn, Kulele returned to the pig sty to put on his false skin.

But Princess Lolee was waiting for him.

"So, you're the handsome man I danced with. Why were you pretending all this time?" she asked.

"I am sorry, my dear wife. I put on the false skin to test if your love was real," Kulele said.

Princess Lolee presented Kulele to her father, who was, of course, delighted. The king blessed their marriage and they moved back to the palace.

Every night when the moon appeared, Kulele would play his magical flute for his beautiful wife and princess with the most gracious heart.

And their days were filled with happiness and they lived happily ever after.

Jordan Dean

VINEWAEWAEYA

Long, long ago in the inlands of Fergusson Island, in a place called Salakadi, there lived a woman called Vinewaewaeya. She had married a handsome man and they lived happily together.

As the years went by, Vinewaewaeya grew old and her youthful beauty faded. As a result, her husband lost interest in her and married a much younger woman as his second wife.

Vinewaewaeya worked like a slave every day. She cleaned the house, swept around the yard and cooked their meals. Vinewaewaeya was heartbroken but never showed it.

One day, Vinewaewaeya scraped coconut in a bowl and told her son to follow her to the river. Her son sat quietly on a rock and watched.

Vinewaewaeya swam to the waterfall, squeezed the coconut juice over herself. She scrubbed her body with a flat stone and the old skin peeled off. A young woman of great beauty appeared.

Vinewaewaeya and her son returned to the village and cooked their meal. She then told her son to cover the door with a coconut woven mat.

Vinewaewaeya's husband and his second wife were working in their garden. Her husband didn't feel well.

"Let's go back to the village," he said to his second wife.

Her husband arrived with his second wife and threw a bundle of firewood in front of the house.

"Here is your firewood. You old, ugly woman," he complained.

Vinewaewaeya heard him but didn't respond. When her husband removed the coconut mat from the door, he got the shock of his life. There before him stood the most beautiful woman he had ever seen. She shone like the stars in the night sky. He stood there speechless.

Vinewaewaeya walked out of the house and headed towards the river. Her husband and son followed. When Vinewaewaeya reached the river, she told her son to sit on the rock again. She dived into the river and surfaced a fair distance away.

"Can you see me?" she asked.

"Yes Mama, I can see you," her son answered.

Vinewaewaeya dived again and surfaced further away.

"Can you see me?" she asked.

"Yes Mama, I can see you," her son replied.

Vinewaewaeya dived again for the third time. She surfaced a great distance away.

"Can you see me?" she asked.

"Yes Mama, I can still see your hair," her son answered.

Vinewaewaeya squeezed some leaves to make the water turn black. Then she sank and disappeared. Her husband jumped into the river to search for her but never found Vinewaewaeya.

And that is why the river at Salakadi is black like the night sky.

MALAKOKOSI

Long, long ago when our ancestors were cannibals, there lived a woman called Malakokosi. She lived with her husband in a small village called Aodebana. Beside their house was a small shelter where the skulls of dead people were kept.

One day, Malakokosi collected coconut leaves, bundled them and left them to dry in the sun.

When it was dark, she called out to her husband.

"Taubada?"

"Yes….," a skull responded.

"Bring a basket and let's go look for eels and prawns," Malakosisi said.

The skull transformed into a man and followed Malakokosi down to the river. Since it was dark, she thought it was her husband.

Each time Malakokosi caught an eel or prawns, she would give it to the skull man to put it into the coconut basket. But the skull man ate the eel or prawns and loaded stones into the basket instead.

They continued upstream until they came to a junction where the river divided. Malakokosi stopped to rest for a while.

"Taubada, let me see the basket and remove the eels waste," she said.

The skull man gave her the basket without saying a word. Malakokosi looked into the basket and saw only stones. She realised that the person she came with was not her husband but something else.

She lit a bundle of coconut leaves and said to the skull man:

"You stay here. I'll check the river on the right side for prawns before we decide which side to follow."

Malakokosi followed the river on the right hand side, pretending to look for prawns. When she turned a corner, she ran back to the village.

The next day, Malakokosi's husband asked her. "Where are the eels and prawns that you caught?"

Malakokosi explained what had happened the previous night.

But her husband didn't believe her. He became suspicious and thought that she went out with another man. For months, they argued about the skull man. Her husband beat Malakokosi frequently and life became miserable for her.

After some time, she couldn't take it anymore. So she followed the river upstream until she came to a place where the water was deep. She jumped into the deep river and changed into a rock.

To this day, the deep part of the river at Aodebana is called Malakokosi.

THE BAGI SNAKE

There once lived a giant snake on a small coral island called Lauwa, just off the coast of Iyaupolo village. The giant snake was special because it excreted shells that were used to make *bagi* necklaces.

An old woman and her granddaughter also lived on Lauwa Island. Every day, the old woman secretly carried a clay pot full of cooked food to the cave where the giant snake lived and placed it on a flat rock at the cave's entrance. She would then call the giant snake to come out to have its meal.

One day, the old woman fell very ill and couldn't walk. She instructed her granddaughter to cook some food in a clay pot.

"My granddaughter, take this food to the cave in the middle of the island," she said. "Place the clay pot on a flat rock and call your great grandfather to come out to have his meal."

The young woman placed the clay pot on her head and set off. She had never seen her great grandfather and was thrilled. When she arrived at the cave, she put the clay pot on the flat rock and called out to her great grandfather just as her grandmother had instructed. She waited anxiously.

The island shook when the giant snake came out of the cave. It was a scaly-looking beast with two huge tusks that protruded on both sides of its mouth.

The young woman screamed and ran away. All along; she had been thinking that her great grandfather was a human being, just like all other grandfathers and great grandfathers.

The giant snake was very upset and appeared in the old woman's dream. The giant snake said, "My great granddaughter has rejected me. I can't live here any more so I am leaving."

That night, lightning flashed and thunder roared. Rain poured down heavily and the place was covered with darkness. The island shook as the giant snake made its way out to sea.

The giant snake swam far away to a distant island called Rossel. And that's why; the people of Rossel Island produce *bagi* necklaces today. There is a snake like passage at Rossel Island too. It's called the 'Snake Passage'.

TAPULUPULU

Once upon a time, there lived a giant called Tapulupulu who had no arms and legs. He lived with his grandchildren in a small village near the beach. Every time when the tide was low, everyone would go down to the reefs and collect shells to cook. Tapulupulu would sit and watch in remorse. He couldn't walk like everyone else.

One morning, Tapulupulu told his grandchildren to remove the skin of a slippery tree and place them on the ground from his house down to the sea. His grandchildren did as they were told. Then, Tapulupulu told them to roll him onto the bark of the slippery tree. Again, his grandchildren did as they were told.

"Thank you my *bubus*. I want to taste the sea and look for shells like everyone else," he said.

When the children released him, Tapulupulu slid along the bark and ended up at the reefs. He was so excited. He ate the sea weeds, shells, small fish and even the reefs. He ate and ate until his stomach was so full.

Around midday, the tide started rising and the villagers returned to the village. Tapulupulu couldn't move. He was also too heavy for his grandchildren to lift. The tide carried Tapulupulu to the roots of a big mangrove tree. He slept there.

The mangrove tree was the home of a sea giant who was away on a trading expedition to the nearby islands.

The sea giant returned the next day with his sailing canoe filled with food, clay pots, arm shells, necklaces and pigs.

Tapulupulu was terrified of him and kept quiet.

The sea giant pulled his canoe ashore. He was thirsty so he took a sling from his basket, loaded a rock and swung it at a coconut tree. Down came a bunch of young coconuts. He swung again and another bunch of young coconuts fell.

Tapulupulu called out.

"Oh my friend! You are so strong!"

The sea giant was startled when he saw Tapulupulu. But his pride got the better of him.

"That's nothing. Watch while I break the trunk," he said and swung the third time.

The coconut tree broke in half and fell.

"My friend, you are the strongest man I've ever seen," Tapulupulu praised him.

"Of course I am!" the sea giant boasted.

The sea giant husked the coconuts and drank the fresh juice. He husked another coconut and gave it to Tapulupulu to drink.

While the sea giant was resting, Tapulupulu asked him. "My friend, I've seen how strong and powerful you are. There is no one to match you. Can I borrow your arms and legs so I can try the sling shot too?"

"Sure, you can have my arms and legs to try. Let's see if you will match my strength!" the sea giant replied.

The sea giant removed his legs and hands and handed them Tapulupulu.

Tapulupulu put them on. He loaded a rock into the sling and swung it at another coconut tree. A bunch of green coconuts fell down.

"Ah, my friend. You are strong too but still can't match me. Try again!" the sea giant said.

Tapulupulu loaded another rock and swung it again. Another bunch of coconuts fell.

"Oh, you still can't match me. Try to break the trunk of the coconut tree in half like I did," the sea giant said.

Tapulupulu loaded the third rock and swung it again. The coconut tree broke in half and fell. The sea giant was now angry that Tapulupulu had matched him.

"Give me back my arms and legs now!" the sea giant yelled.

Tapulupulu laughed at him. "My friend, for years I had no arms and legs to move around. They are mine now. You can stay here and drown."

Tapulupulu left the sea giant and returned to the village. Everyone was surprised that he had arms and legs now. Tapulupulu told them about how he tricked the proud sea giant.

That evening, the villagers helped Tapulupulu to carry all the food, clay pots, arm shells, necklaces and pigs from the sailing canoe up to the village and they had a big feast that night.

Meanwhile, back at the mangrove tree, the tide came in and the proud sea giant drowned.

Jordan Dean

MANUKAPWATAYATAYA

Many years ago, there lived a monster pig called Buluwagalagala on Normanby Island. Buluwagalagala attacked every village, killing and eating the people. Everyone on the island lived in great fear.

After some time, the people decided to move to another island called Ware. They prepared two big sailing canoes and sailed off for Ware Island.

They left one woman behind because she had sores all over her body. She hid in a cave. She mated with a creature that lives in the trees and gave birth to a son called Manukapwatayataya. His younger brother was a dog.

Manukapwatayataya grew up to be a strong and brave young man. His mother warned him to avoid the mountains because Buluwagalagala lived there.

The coast was also dangerous because a giant octopus lived there.

Manukapwatayataya was exploring the island one evening when the ground suddenly shook. He quickly hid in the bushes and waited. Buluwagalagala came down from the mountains and vomited all sorts of food out into the sea. At this, all the tuna fish came up to feast on the food.

Buluwagalagala watched his fish eat then returned to the mountains. Manukapwatayataya came out from his hiding place and speared some of the tuna fish. Manukapwatayataya's mother was afraid to cook the tuna.

"Where did you catch these tuna? Aren't these Buluwagalagala's fish?" she asked.

"Don't worry, Mama. Just cook the tuna for dinner," Manukapwatayataya replied.

Every day, Manukapwatayataya would hide and wait for Buluwagalagala to feed his fish. When Buluwagalagala left, Manukapwatayataya would spear the tuna. This went on until he speared all the tuna.

One evening, Manukapwatayataya told his mother and brother that he wanted to kill Buluwagalagala.

"You must be careful, son," his mother said.

Manukapwatayataya cut down the palm trees and sharpened seven bundles of spears. He then built seven platforms starting from the mountain where Buluwagalagala lived down to the cave where they lived. He placed a bundle of spears on each platform. At the entrance of their cave, Manukapwatayataya placed a double pointed spear.

Early the next day, Manukapwatayataya planted a flower in front of the cave.

"Watch this flower. If the petals fall then you know I am gone. But if the flower is still intact then I am still alive," he told his mother.

Manukapwatayataya and his brother left for the mountains. When they got there, they climbed onto the first platform and rested. Manukapwatayataya took out his sling, loaded a stone and swung it at Buluwagalagala's nest.

"Ah, who is this trying to destroy my nest?" Buluwagalagala cried out.

Manukapwatayataya loaded another stone and swung again it at Buluwagalagala's nest.

"Ah, I've eaten everyone on Normanby Island. Who the hell are you to destroy my nest?" Buluwagalagala shouted.

"Yes, it is true you've eaten everyone. But you haven't eaten Manukapwatayataya!"

Buluwagalagala was furious and charged at Manukapwatayataya. Manukapwatayataya threw as many spears as he could but Buluwagalagala was so strong and broke the platform. His brother bit Buluwagalagala on the leg while Manukapwatayataya jumped to the next platform.

The fight continued on the different platforms until Manukapwatayataya reached the entrance of their cave. He grabbed the double pointed spear and killed Buluwagalagala.

Manukapwatayataya asked his mother again: "Mama, are there any more monsters around?"

"Oh my son, there's a giant eagle on the other side of our island that eats people," his mother replied.

The next day, Manukapwatayataya made a canoe with two holes on it and sailed around the island. The giant eagle was sitting in its nest on a cliff. Manukapwatayataya took out his sling, loaded a stone and swung it at the eagles nest. The stone destroyed the giant eagles nest.

"Ah, I've eaten everyone here on Normanby Island. Who are you to destroy my nest?" the giant eagle shouted.

"Yes, it is true you've eaten everyone. But you haven't eaten Manukapwatayataya!"

Upon seeing Manukapwatayataya, the giant eagle flew down to kill him. Manukapwatayataya quickly dived into the sea and turned the canoe over. The giant eagle stood on the canoe, looking for Manukapwatayataya.

Manukapwatayataya reached out and quickly tied the giant eagle's legs together and then surfaced. The giant eagle couldn't fly because its legs were tied to the canoe.

He beat the giant eagle with his club until it lay dead. Manukapwatayataya then loaded the dead eagle and sailed back to show his mother. His mother was so happy to see him return alive.

Manukapwatayataya asked his mother again: "Mama, are there any more monsters around?"

"Oh my son, there's the giant octopus that is still living on our shore," his mother replied.

"I will kill the octopus tomorrow!" he said.

"Be careful, son. The octopus has ten lives. It will discharge ten times. You must take cover and don't let it touch you," his mother warned.

The next day, Manukapwatayataya went down to the beach and speared the octopus. He quickly hid under a rock. The octopus discharged muck nine times. Manukapwatayataya mistook it as the tenth discharge and came out of his hiding place. Just then the giant octopus gave out its last discharge which burnt Manukapwatayataya's left eye.

Back at the cave, Manukapwatayataya's mother saw a petal fall from the flower. She knew her son was wounded. The octopus finally lay dead and Manukapwatayataya returned to the cave. For a week, his mother nursed the wound on his face until it healed.

Manukapwatayataya then made a small canoe. He used the giant eagle's feather as a sail and attached Buluwagalagala's huge hip bone as the steer.

Manukapwatayataya sent the canoe to Ware Island as a sign to the relatives there.

The people at Ware Island were surprised to see the small canoe with the giant eagle's feather and Buluwagalagala's hip bone. They knew that the monsters on Normanby Island were gone but wondered who killed them. Finally, one of the elders stood up.

"Remember the woman with sores all over her body? I think she had a son who killed the monsters," he said.

Some of the men sailed back to Normanby Island to check if the place was now safe. When the men arrived, they were surprised to find Manukapwatayataya's mother. She requested a bride for her warrior son when they returned.

And so the people returned to Normanby Island. Manukapwatayataya married a beautiful lady and they lived happily ever after.

Jordan Dean

TAUKEDUWAIWAI

Long ago in our ancestors time, there was little boy and his sister. They lived in a small hamlet. Everyone, including their parents had been killed and eaten by a giant called Taukeduwaiwai.

One day, Taukeduwai captured the two children but didn't eat them straight away.

"My *bubus*, let's go look for fish and shells at an island," he said.

The children were afraid of Taukeduwaiwai.

"*Bubu*, we can come but we didn't prepare any food, young coconuts and fetch water to take with us," the boy said.

"My *bubus*, don't worry about anything. There's food, young coconuts and water on the canoe. Come my *bubus*. Get on and let's go," Taukeduwaiwai said.

The children boarded the canoe and they sailed to a faraway island. When they got to the island, Taukeduwaiwai sat on the sand and chewed betel nut.

"My *bubus*, go around the island and look for fish and shells. Make sure to fill your baskets before we sail back to our hamlet," he said to the children.

The children set off for the reefs on the other side of the island. The tide was low and there were lots of fish and shells on the reefs. The boy speared the fish that were trapped in the shallow waters. His sister collected oysters, clam shells and other edible shells.

By noon, their baskets were full. The boy lifted a basket and placed it on his sister's head, then placed the other basket on his shoulder. They slowly made their way back to the canoe. When they came around the point, Taukeduwaiwai pulled the canoe into the water and paddled out to the deep.

The children ran as fast as they could and cried out: "*Bubu*, wait for us. Please don't leave us on this island."

"Sorry my *bubus*, I can't take you back. Stay here and be eaten by the witches that live on this island," Taukeduwaiwai told them.

Taukeduwaiwai sailed off for another island leaving the children on the beach. The little girl continued crying while her brother comforted her.

They sat on the sand and watched the canoe until it disappeared. The sun was setting over the horizon.

The children were hungry. They sat wondering how to make a fire to cook the fish and shells. Back home, they would rub a special stick to make fire.

When darkness arrived, a fire suddenly appeared at the point that they had passed earlier.

"Look sister, there's a fire. You stay here. I'll go and ask for a few burning sticks so we can cook," the boy said.

The little boy headed in the direction of the fire. When he got to the fire, there was no one in sight. He pulled out a few burning sticks. Suddenly, a woman's voice cried out: "That hurts! That's my eyes that you're poking!"

The little boy dropped the fire sticks in fear. "I am sorry, *bubu*. I thought it was an ordinary fire so I removed some stick to make my own fire," he said.

An old woman appeared and said: "Go back to your sister. Walk up a little distance and there's a hut nearby that has a fire burning. Go there and cook your fish and shells."

The old woman disappeared and the little boy returned to his sister. He told her about the fire and the old lady.

"I am scared. Taukeduwaiwa said that the witches on this island will eat us," the little girl said.

"We have no choice but to trust the old women," the boy said.

Still afraid, the children walked up slowly in the direction that the old woman had instructed.

Lo and behold, there was a hut with a burning fire. The old woman that appeared earlier to the little boy was sitting beside the fire. She welcomed the children and cooked their fish and shells with some bananas and yam.

The children told the old women about how the giant, Taukeduwaiwai left them to be eaten by witches on this island. The old women felt sorry for the children.

"Don't worry. You're safe with me. But where is that giant?" she asked.

"He sailed off to another island," the boy said.

After dinner, the little girl was so tired and fell asleep. The boy stayed awake until day break. He feared that the old woman might eat them. But nothing happened to them that night. They stayed with the old woman while waiting for Taukeduwaiwai to return.

After a week, the children saw a sailing canoe approaching. They knew it was Taukeduwaiwai's canoe. The old woman gave the boy a black stick and the little girl, a bird.

She instructed the children.

"When the canoe arrives, go greet the giant and be nice to him. When it's time for him to sail off, get on with him and let the bird go. Then tell the giant to catch it for you. When he jumps off the canoe to get the bird, leave him behind."

"What will I do with this stick?" the boy asked.

"The giant will try his best to get back onto the canoe. Point the stick at him and it will scare him away."

Then the old woman and the hut disappeared. Taukeduwaiwai was surprised to see the children.

"Oh, my *bubus*! So you're still alive? I thought the witches had eaten you," he said. "Let me rest before we sail back home."

At noon, they pulled the canoe down to sail off. The little girl let the bird go as instructed by the old woman. The bird flew back to the shore.

"My *bubu*, please catch my bird before we leave," the little girl begged Taukeduwaiwai.

Taukeduwaiwai went after the bird. When he got closer, the bird flew away. He continued following the bird until he was some miles away from the canoe. The children quickly paddled out to the deep and pulled down the sail.

Taukeduwaiwai finally caught the bird and headed back for the canoe. To his dismay, he saw that the children were about to sail off.

"My *bubus*, please wait for me," he called to them.

"You left us on this island. Now, we'll leave you here for the witches to eat you," the boy said.

Taukeduwaiwai quickly climbed a tall coconut tree and bent it down towards the canoe so he could jump on board. Just as Taukeduwaiwai was about to jump, the little boy pointed the black stick at him. Taukeduwaiwai was terrified and sprung back to the shore. He sat on the sand begging the children to return for him. The children waved at him and sailed back home.

Taukeduwaiwai collected several logs and placed them around him in a circle. He built a bon-fire at the centre. When the place was dark, Taukeduwaiwai saw strange lights appear around him. He knew they were witches. So he pretended that he was not alone.

"Hey sleepy heads, wake up! Why are you sleeping? Wake up and put more wood on the fire!" he shouted at the logs

Taukeduwaiwai tried all sorts to ideas to scare the witches away. Eventually, the witches captured him. That night, the witches killed Taukeduwaiwai and feasted on his corpse.

VINENAWATA

Long, long ago, there lived a woman called Vinenawata. She grew up in a village called Lomenai on Fergusson Island. She then got married and settled at Bwalelei. She gave birth to a daughter and named her Maduwai. Maduwai grew up to be a beautiful young woman.

One day, a feast was held at Lomenai. But Vinenawata had no pig to contribute. An evil thought came into her mind: 'Maduwai will be my pig.'

And so; Vinenawata loaded her canoe with food and she and Maduwai paddled towards Lomenai. Maduwai suspected that she will be eaten. When they reached Moduya point, Maduwai cried out:

Vinenawata nuvunuvumi aipono pono piyo piyo…

Vinenawata's pig. I am not a pig. I am human…

"Stop crying Maduwai! Paddle on. My brothers are waiting," Vinenawata said.

Maduwai paddled on. When they reached Waleta Point, Maduwai cried again:

Vinenawata nuvunuvumi aipono pono piyo piyo…
Vinenawata's pig. I am not a pig, I am human…

"Stop crying Maduwai. Paddle on. My brothers are waiting," Vinenawata said.

Maduwai paddled on until they reached Lomenai. The villagers carried the food up to the village. They placed Maduwai on a flat rock. Maduwai continued crying while her uncle's prepared the food and greens for the feast.

When the food and greens were prepared, they killed Maduwai and cut her up into pieces. They distributed the pieces among themselves.

"My teeth are not strong so I want the heart," Maduwai's grandmother requested.

Maduwai's uncles cooked their pieces. However Maduwai's grandmother didn't cook her heart. Instead, she placed it in a clay pot with some water and covered it up.

She then cast a spell and Maduwai came back to life.

The villagers made huge fires but their food and protein would not cook. Maduwai's grandmother called Vinenawata over to her hut and said:

"Go raise a pig and give it to your brothers! Not your daughter!"

She then called Maduwai to come out of the clay pot. Vinenawata bowed her head in shame. She returned back to Bwalelei and raised a pig to pay for her shame.

Maduwai stayed with her grandmother. She never wanted to see her wicked mother again.

BUWAWANA – LEGEND OF THE MERMAID

A long time ago, there lived a beautiful girl called Buwawana. She lived with her father and wicked stepmother. Every day she swept around the house, washed the clay pots and cooked food.

One day, her father went out hunting while her stepmother went to the garden. Buwawana was busy sweeping around the house and forgot to check on the food. To her dismay, the food was burnt.

"Oh, no!" she sighed. "How will I explain this my step mother?"

Her step-mother returned from the garden early. Buwawana explained what happened but her wicked stepmother was furious.

"You're a stupid, lazy girl!" she yelled and hit Buwawana with a stick.

"Please forgive me," Buwawana pleaded.

Her step mother continued beating her with a stick until her whole body was red and sore.

Buwawana shed tears in silence and waited for her father. She put on a beautiful grass skirt and wore a long *bagi* on her neck. The sun was setting when her father came home. She carried her coconut basket and walked down to the beach. There she cried:

"Mother where are you now? My life has no meaning. I want to come to you."

She continued walking along the beach. At the end of the beach, she cried again:

"Mother where are you now? My life has no meaning. I want to come to you."

Buwawana climbed onto a fallen tree that stretched out to the sea. She reached the tip of the tree and cried the third time:

"Mother where are you now? My life has no meaning. I want to come to you."

By then her father heard Buwawana's cry and followed her.

"Wait for me, my daughter," he called after her.

She sat and waited until her father was within an arm's length. When he reached out to hold her, she jumped into the sea and transformed into a mermaid.

Buwawana waved back at her weeping father and swam out to the deep blue sea. She was never seen again.

GLOSSARY OF TERMS USED

Bagi	Shell necklace
Bubu	Grandfather / Grandchild
Kundu	Traditional drum
Singsing	Traditional celebration

ABOUT THE AUTHOR

Jordan Dean was born on June 12, 1984 on Fergusson Island, Milne Bay Province, Papua New Guinea. He completed his primary and secondary education in Alotau, MBP, PNG. He has a degree in accounting and management.

His story *'Gabubu – Legend of the White Dove'* was the winner of the Heritage Writing category for the Crocodile Literature Prize in 2017.

He is the author of *'Forbidden Dancer: A Collection of Poems'*, *'Reluctant Bride & other Short Stories from Papua New Guinea'* and a short novel *'Tama'gega – Fatherless Child'*. The books are all available on Amazon.